I'M A LEEDS UNITED SUPERFAN!

GW00535709

THE OFFICIAL
Leeds United
ANNUAL 2015

Written by John Wray

Photography:
Andrew Varley Picture Agency

Great Northern Books
PO Box 213, Ilkley, LS29 9WS
www.greatnorthernbooks.co.uk

© Leeds United FC

Design and layout: David Burrill

ISBN: 978-0-9928193-5-4

CIP Data
A catalogue for this book is available from the British Library

GREAT NORTHERN

£8

Contents

New faces   5
Our top sharp-shooters down the years   12
Name the countries   20
Rodolph Austin   22
Leeds Legend: Jack Charlton   23
Quiz: World Cup Facts - True or False   24
Alex Mowatt: Young Player of the Year   26
Quiz: What do you know about Italy?   28
Neil Redfern: proud of his
Academy whites   30
Phil Beeton - United's Super Fan   32
Quiz: Summing up the squad   34
Perils of being a manager   36
Diary of a season   38
Spot the Difference   45
Player profile: Charlie Taylor   46
Q&A with Billy Sharp   48
Nicky Ajose: My favourite things   53
United's best ever – Do you agree?   54
Leeds United's Family Award   56
Mirco Antenucci   57
Eddie Gray top of the class   58
Quiz: Have you been paying attention?   60
Wordsearch: Find the captains?   61
Colour-in Liam Cooper   62
Answers to quizzes   63

New faces look to make their mark

THE summer of 2014, up to transfer deadline day, was one of the busiest on record for Leeds United as the list of new signings moved well into double figures.

After the disappointment of finishing 15th in the Championship and parting with manager Brian McDermott, a major team rebuilding job was launched, with players arriving from home and abroad and others taking the exit door.

Among senior players leaving were Ross McCormack, Michael Brown, Danny Pugh, Paul Green, Luke Varney, El-Hadji Diouf, Adam Drury, Jamie Ashdown, Lee Peltier, Cameron Stewart, Marius Zaliukas, Tom Lees, Dominic Poleon and Matt Smith, while six Academy players also left: Simon Lenighan, Nathan Turner, Lewis Turner, Richard Bryan, Smith Tiesse and Gboly Ariyibi. In addition, head coach David Hockaday paid for a poor start to the 2014-15 season by losing his job.

First to arrive was STUART TAYLOR, the former Arsenal, Aston Villa and Manchester City goalkeeper whose contract at Reading had ended. Taylor, born in Romford on November 28, 1980, has spent much of his career as an understudy and had loan spells at Bristol Rovers, Crystal Palace, Peterborough, Leicester City, Cardiff City and US Palermo. Stuart is a former England Under 21 international.

He signed a one-year contract at Elland Road and made his competitive debut for United in the 2-1 victory over Accrington Stanley in the Capital One Cup on August 12, 2014.

On his arrival from Chievo, MARCO SILVESTRI was handed the No1 squad number, which suggested he would be first choice goalkeeper. Born at Castelnovo ne' Monti, Italy, on March 2, 1981, Silvestri is an ex Italy Under 21 international. After playing youth football at

MARCO SILVESTRI

Modena he joined Chievo and was loaned to Reggiana, Padova and Cagliari.

Signed a four-year contract and made his competitive debut for United in the 2-0 defeat at Millwall on August 9, 2014.

French striker SOULEYMANE DOUKARA made a rapid impact on his home debut, scoring two top quality goals in the opening 38 minutes against Accrington Stanley in the Capital One Cup, having played his first competitive game for the club a few days earlier at Millwall.

Doukara, who was born in Meudon, France, on September 29, 1991, joined United on a season-long loan from Catania with a view to a permanent deal. His nickname is Dudu. He played youth football at SCM Chatillon, CA Paris, Paris Universite Club and AC Milan (on trial). His senior clubs have been Rovigo, Grasshopper Zurich (on trial), Vibonese, Catania and Juve Stabia (loan).

Midfielder TOMMASO BIANCHI joined the club on a four-year contract from Serie A club Sassuolo. Born in Piombino, Italy, on November 1, 1988, Tommaso is an ex Italy Under 21 international. Spent his youth career at Follonica and Piacenza. Became a senior player at Piacenza before joining Chievo on loan, failing to play a single game with them. He was more successful at his next club Sassuolo, winning promotion to Serie A but then being loaned to Modena who lost in the semi-finals of the promotion play-offs. On joining Leeds he missed the opening league game of the season at Millwall through a suspension carried over from the previous season in Italy but made his debut in the Capital One Cup win against Accrington.

GAETANO BERARDI, a mobile, hard-tackling right back, was born in Sorengo, Switzerland, on August 21, 1988. The Swiss international signed a two-year contract when he moved from Sampdoria. He started his youth career at Lugano before moving to Brescia where he made over 100 senior appearances and won promotion to Serie A in 2009-10. Brescia were relegated the following season but in 2012 Berardi joined his former Brescia manager Giuseppe Lachini at Sampdoria where he gained another promotion to Serie A in 2011-12.

Towards the end of an impressive debut for United in their Capital One Cup-tie against Accrington he was sent off for a rash tackle and was handed a three-match ban for dangerous play.

Attacking midfielder ZAN BENEDICIC also made his Leeds debut against Accrington, replacing fellow youngster Lewis Cook in the 65th minute. Born in Kranj, Slovenia, on October 3, 1995, Benedicic joined United on a season-long loan from AC Milan. He played youth football at Triglav Kranj and AC Milan before being included in Milan's senior squad, though he has yet to

TOMMASO
BIANCHI

SOULEYMANE DOUKARA

NICKY AJOSE

make a first team appearance for them. He flew home from Milan's tour to the USA in July amid rumours that he was about to join Leeds.

Striker or winger NICKY AJOSE (full name Nicholas Olushola Ajose) was born in Bury on October 7, 1991, and signed a three-year contract on joining United from Peterborough. He was a trainee at Manchester United but never played for the Reds' first team before joining Peterborough. He had two spells on loan at Bury and also went on loan to Scunthorpe, Chesterfield, Crawley Town and Swindon. He has played for England Under 16s and Under 17s but is also eligible for Nigeria. Was named League One Player of the Month in January, 2014, and made his Leeds debut at Millwall on the opening day of the 2014-15 season.

BILLY SHARP, a proven goal-scorer, had long been linked with a move to Elland Road before finally moving from Southampton on August 13, 2014. The Sheffield-born striker entered the world on February 5, 1986, and always wanted to be a footballer. Started out at Middlewood Rovers Junior Club and played for the youth teams at Rotherham and Sheffield United before breaking into the Blades' first team. He went on loan to Rushden & Diamonds and after a successful spell at Scunthorpe, where he scored a club record 30 league goals in 2006-7, he re-joined Sheffield United for £2million. A loan move to Doncaster became permanent and after helping Southampton into the Premier League he was loaned by the Saints to Nottingham Forest, Reading and Doncaster again. Signed a two-year contract at Leeds and celebrated his debut with a goal in the 1-0 win over Middlesbrough at Elland Road, a match televised live by Sky.

Central defender GIUSEPPE BELLUSCI, who initially joined on a one-year loan deal from Catania but quickly agreed a four-year contract, was born in Trebisacce, Italy, on August 21, 1989. The former Italy Under 21 international was nicknamed The Warrior by fans of Catania where he made 99 domestic appearances. He rose through the ranks at Ascoli, making his Serie A debut for them aged 17. Helped Catania set a club record 56 points from 38 Serie A games in season 2012-13 but Catania were relegated after finishing third from bottom in 2013-14. Bellusci's Leeds debut was delayed by the

BILLY SHARP

9

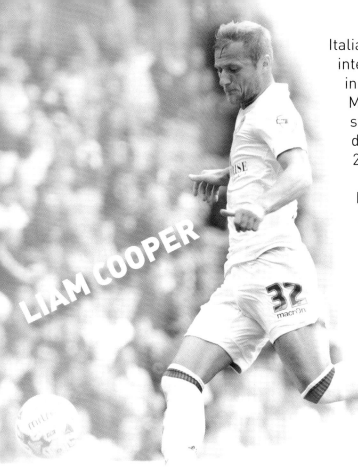

LIAM COOPER

Italian Bank Holiday as his international clearance failed to arrive in time to allow him to play against Middlesbrough at Elland Road. Was sent off on his United debut in a 4-1 defeat at Millwall on August 23, 2014.

Central defender or left back LIAM COOPER, born in Hull on August 30, 1991, cost United around £600,000 from Chesterfield after two previous offers had been rejected. He joined his home town club at the age of 12 and progressed through the ranks into the first team. The Tigers loaned him to Carlisle, Huddersfield and Chesterfield before his move to the Spireites became permanent. He helped Chesterfield to the League Two title in 2013-14 and was named in the PFA divisional team of the year.

Cooper is a former Scotland Under-19 international who made his Leeds debut in the 1-0 win over Middlesbrough on August 16, 2014.

Striker MIRCO ANTENUCCI, who played for nine clubs in Italy, arrived at Leeds on August 20, 2014, from Serie B side Ternana Calcio where he was captain. Antenucci, born on September 8, 1984, agreed a two-year contract. He scored 19 goals in 40 games for Ternana in 2013-14, netting a special goal against Spezia in March, 2014. After controlling the ball on his chest he scored with a spectacular bicycle kick. His best season was 2009-10 when he scored 24 goals in 40 games while on loan at Ascoli. Made his United debut at Millwall on August 23, 2014.

Danish international attacking midfielder CASPER SLOTH, aged 22, was born in Aarhus and began his youth

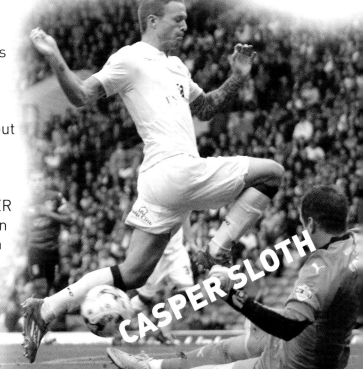

CASPER SLOTH

career with Brabrand IF. He joined the AGF Aarhus academy in 2004, making his debut in the Danish Superliga championship in December, 2009, aged 17. AGF were relegated in 2013-14 but Sloth was rated one of his country's most promising young talents. On his arrival at Elland Road on August 25, 2014, he agreed a three year contract and made his debut in the 1-0 home win against Bolton on August 30.

Another highly promising attacking midfield player, Brazilian ADRYAN OLIVEIRA TAVARES, 20, joined the club before August was out. Known simply as Adryan, he was born in Rio de Janeiro on August 10, 1994, and came through the youth ranks into Flamengo's first team, making 37 senior appearances. A thigh injury restricted him to just five games while on loan at Cagliari and he joined Leeds on a season-long loan with a view to a permanent transfer. In Brazil the free-kick specialist was nicknamed 'heir of Zico' and 'the new Zico'.

Still they kept arriving, 19-year-old centre-back DARIO DEL FABRO becoming the club's 14th summer signing when he joined on a season-long loan from Cagliari. Del Fabro had intended playing on loan for Serie B side Delfino Pescara from August 3, 2014, but the loan was terminated so he could come to Leeds instead. Born on March 24, 1995, in Alghero, Italy, Del Fabro is a product of Cagliari's youth set-up.

Signing number 15 was winger or striker BRIAN MONTENEGRO on a season-long loan. The former Paraguay Under-20 international arrived on September 1, 2014, from Nacional Asuncion. Montenegro was loaned to West Ham during 2011-12.

MIRCO ANTENUCCI

Our top sharp-shooters down the years

ALLAN Clarke cost Leeds United a then British club record £165,000 when he joined the club from Leicester City in the summer of 1969.

The cash paid proved a sound investment as pencil-slim England striker Clarke went on to top the club's goal-scoring charts for four seasons. Since then, only Australian international Mark Viduka has done the same.

Lee Chapman, David Healy and Jermaine Beckford finished top scorer three times each, with Beckford the last player to top 30 goals in a season in all competitions. Although Beckford scored 34 times to finish top scorer in 2009, David Healy needed just seven goals to finish on top in 2006.

Here are our top marksmen over the last 44 years and the number of goals they scored to top the pile.

Allan Clarke

1970 – 26 goals (joint)
1971 – 23
1973 – 26
1975 – 22

Mick Jones
1970 – 26 (joint)
1974 – 17

Peter Lorimer
1972 - 28

Duncan McKenzie
1976 – 17

Joe Jordan
1977 - 12

13

Ray Hankin
1978 – 21

John Hawley
1979 – 17

Kevin Hird
1980 – 8

Carl Harris
1981 – 10

14

Arthur Graham
1982 – 9

Aidan Butterworth
1983 – 13

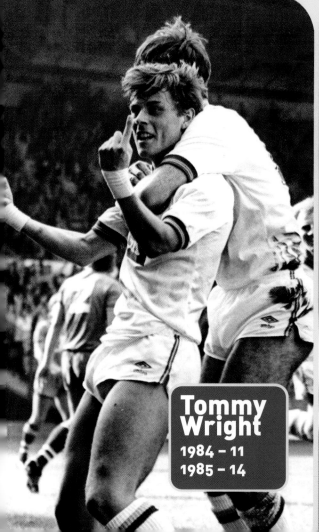

Tommy Wright
1984 – 11
1985 – 14

Ian Baird
1986 – 12
1987 – 19

15

John Sheridan
1988 – 14

Bobby Davison
89 – 17

Gordon Strachan
1990 – 18

Lee Chapman
1991 – 31
1992 – 20
1993 – 19

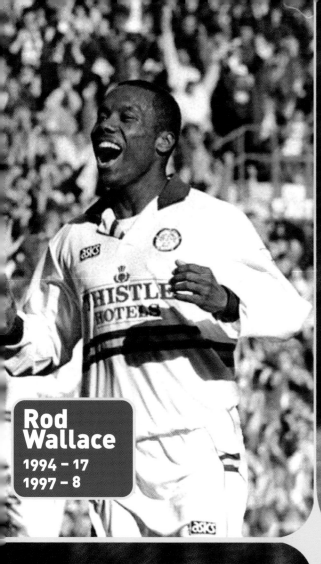

Rod Wallace
1994 – 17
1997 – 8

Tony Yeboah
1995 – 13
1996 – 19

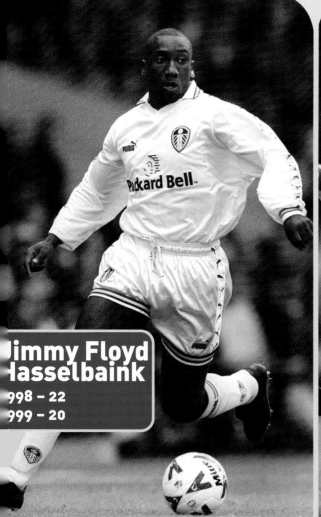

Jimmy Floyd Hasselbaink
998 – 22
999 – 20

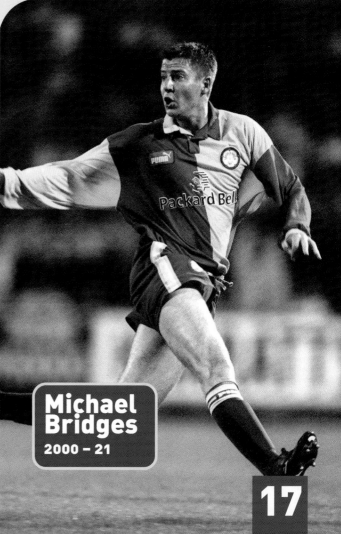

Michael Bridges
2000 – 21

17

Mark Viduka

2001 – 22
2002 – 16
2003 – 22
2004 – 12

David Healy

2005 – 7
2006 – 14 (joint)
2007 – 10

Rob Hulse
2006 – 14 (joint)

Jermaine Beckford
2008 – 20
2009 – 34

Luciano Becchio
2011 – 20
2013 – 19

Ross McCormack
2012 – 19
2014 – 29

Name the countries of their birth

1

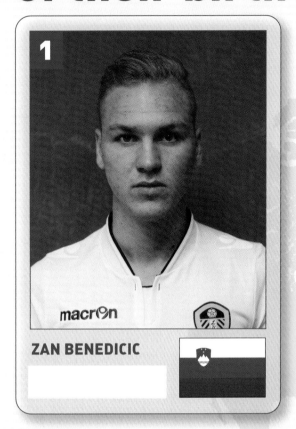

ZAN BENEDICIC

2

GAETANO BERARDI

5

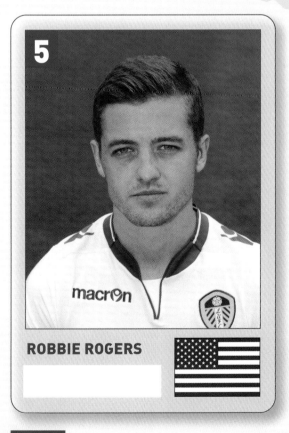

ROBBIE ROGERS

6

KASPER SCHMEICHEL

Players from many countries have turned out for Leeds United over the years. Here is a selection. Can you name the countries where they were born? The clues are in the flags and the answers are on Page 63.

3

GIUSEPPE BELLUSCI

4

SOULEYMANE DOUKARA

7

MAX GRADEL

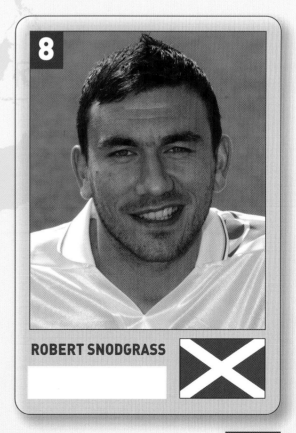

8

ROBERT SNODGRASS

RODOLPH AUSTIN

Big Jack Charlton became a pillar of Leeds United's defence during the Don Revie era and was nicknamed 'The Giraffe'.

Born in Ashington in May, 1935, he spent 23 years as a player at Elland Road, turning out in more games than anyone in the club's history. Jack made 629 league appearances and 773 in all competitions, helping the club to the Second Division title (1964), First Division title (1969), FA Cup (1972), League Cup (1968), Charity Shield (1969) and Inter-Cities Fairs Cup (1968 and 1971).

He and his younger brother Bobby were World Cup winners with England in 1966 and Jack wore the England shirt 35 times.

After leaving Leeds he managed Middlesbrough, Sheffield Wednesday, Newcastle United and the Republic of Ireland.

JACK CHARLTON

World Cup Facts

True or False?

1	Germany won the tournament for a fourth time.	T	F
2	Former Leeds United midfielder Alex Sabella coached Brazil at the World Cup.	T	F
3	England played in Group C.	T	F
4	Mario Balotelli scored Italy's first goal in their 2-1 win against England.	T	F
5	Daniel Sturridge scored England's goal against Italy.	T	F
6	The huge statue of Jesus overlooking Rio is called Christ The King.	T	F
7	Brazil's Group game against Mexico was played at Fortaleza, 258 miles from the equator.	T	F
8	Germany and Croatia played in the same Group.	T	F
9	Gary Lineker presented ITV's coverage of the World Cup.	T	F
10	Luis Suarez scored twice against England.	T	F
11	Former Leeds United player James Milner and Ross Barkley, who had a spell on loan at Elland Road, were England team-mates against Costa Rica.	T	F
12	Mario Gotze scored the winning goal in the final.	T	F

ENGLAND bowed out of the 2014 World Cup early, but there were plenty of thrills and spills in the world's most prestigious football tournament. To test your knowledge we've set you a True or False quiz, with the answers on Page 63. Just study these statements and decide whether they are true or false. Some are easy and some more difficult, so impress your pals with the answers.

13 Brazil superstar Neymar wore squad number nine for the tournament. **T** **F**

14 England lost 3-1 to Uruguay. **T** **F**

15 Spain were the holders going into the tournament but bowed out in the Group stage. **T** **F**

16 Robin van Persie scored three goals in Holland's 5-1 win against Spain in Group B. **T** **F**

17 Former Leeds United player Max Gradel played for Ivory Coast at the World Cup. **T** **F**

18 England lost their first two games for the first time in a World Cup finals tournament. **T** **F**

19 Colombia's James Rodrigues scored in all his five games, totalling six goals. **T** **F**

20 Jurgen Klinsmann was the World Cup winners' coach. **T** **F**

21 Hosts Brazil finished in third place. **T** **F**

22 Argentina v Holland was the first semi-final. **T** **F**

24 England went out in the Group stage for the first time since 1958. **T** **F**

23 Germany's Miroslav Klose scored his 16th World Cup goal in the 7-1 semi-final demolition of Brazil to set a new record. **T** **F**

Alex is looking to score more goals

ALEX MOWATT was a popular winner of the Leeds United Young Player of the Year award after making a big impact in his first season of first team football.

The central midfield player from Doncaster is a product of the club's Academy, which he joined at nine years of age, and his progress has delighted his coaches.

Alex made 31 appearances for the first team in 2013-14, showing a maturity beyond his 19 years and attracting a growing army of fans. United's owner Massimo Cellino is keen to see the club's Academy continue to produce a conveyor belt of talent for the first team and Mowatt's progress offers encouragement to others hoping to rise through the ranks.

The man who captained United to the Under 18 Championship in 2012-13, made his senior debut aged 17 against his home-town club Doncaster at the Keepmoat Stadium as the Whites won 3-1 in the Capital One Cup second round. Team-mate Scott Wootton also made his debut and headed one of the goals.

Alex's performance delighted United's then manager Brian McDermott who said after the match: "You can't make a statement like he looked out of place. He was excellent. I had no worries about Alex playing whatsoever. We need to look after him because he is one of our own."

Mowatt's next start came at Newcastle in a 2-0 defeat in the Capital One Cup third round and he kept his place for his league debut in another 2-0 setback at Millwall. A run in the side boosted his confidence and he scored his first senior goal in the 5-1 West Yorkshire derby win over Huddersfield Town at Elland Road on January 2.

Alex said: "Obviously I was proud to win the Young Player of the Year trophy because some big names have won it in the past. I was very happy with my first season in the first team. When you break into the team you have to take your chance and that is what I did."

He was "very surprised" how quickly his debut came along, even though he had played in pre-season at Shelbourne, and facing his home town club at Doncaster made his competitive debut even more special. "It was a good game because we won 3-1 and some

ALEX MOWATT
YOUNG PLAYER OF THE YEAR

of my mates are Donny fans," beamed Alex. "I always look for Doncaster's results, though I am not a Doncaster fan. I am a Leeds fan.

"We played Doncaster three times last season, beating them twice away and losing at Elland Road, and I played in all three."

He admits there are parts of his game he needs to improve, including scoring and creating more goals. "My one goal last season came against Huddersfield and it was a strange day because the manager (Brian McDermott) had been sacked so he wasn't at the game, and he was then given his job back.

"It was a relief to get my first goal because it is frustrating when you are hitting the bar and things like that. I played quite a lot of games last season and want to do the same this time. There have been lots of changes at the club but with hard work we can do well."

What do you know about Italy?

WHEN Massimo Cellino and his family became Leeds United's new owners in April, 2014, they brought a flavour of Italy to Elland Road.

So we've decided to test your knowledge about Massimo's country. Here are some pictures of well-known Italian landmarks. Can you name them? The answers are on Page 63.

Also we have some questions for you to answer. Again the answers are on Page 63.

1 What are the three colours on the Italian flag?

2 Who was the famous Italian artist who painted the Mona Lisa?

3 What is the name of the volcano that erupted in AD 79, burying the Roman cities of Pompei and Herculaneum?

4 What was the name of Italy's currency before the Euro?

5 Which team finished the 2013-14 season as champions of Serie A?

6 Which team's home stadium is the San Siro?

7 What is the capital city of Italy?

8 Former Leeds United midfielder Olivier Dacourt joined which Italian team in 2003?

9 Who coached Italy in the 2014 World Cup?

10 What famous Italian city is also a girl's name?

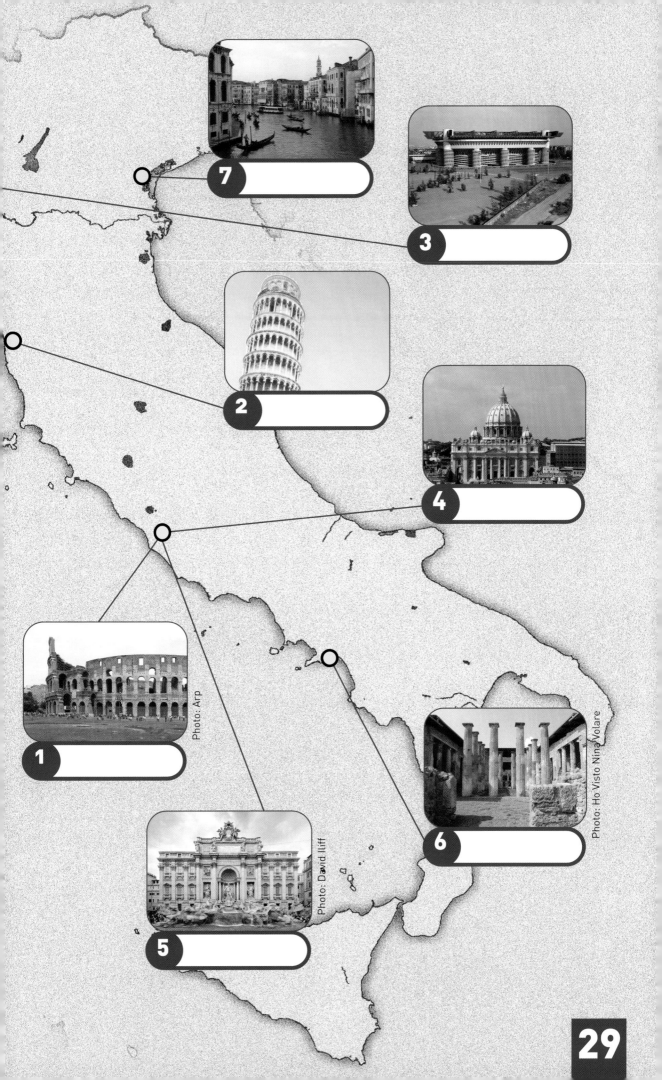

7

3

2

4

Photo: Arp

1

Photo: Ho Visto Nina Volare

6

Photo: David Iliff

5

Neil so proud of his Academy whites

EVERY time a graduate of Leeds United's Academy turns out for the first team, Neil Redfearn wears a smile as wide as Elland Road!

Pride in his young players' achievements is something that comes naturally to the club's Academy Manager and head of coaching, as he is responsible for the development of kids like Sam Byram and Alex Mowatt, who made it all the way from the Under 9's into the first team.

Dewsbury-born Neil has the distinguished record of playing 790 matches in the Football League and over 1,000 first team games in a career spanning 24 years, so naturally he misses the enjoyment of playing competitive football.

"As anyone who has played at a decent level will tell you, there is no substitute for playing, but coaching and developing these kids is the next best thing," he says. "When they come to the club they are a blank canvas. They want to do well and you feel a responsibility to them.

"When you see them pull on that white shirt at Elland Road it's a great feeling. Sometimes we pinch ourselves and say 'that's Sam Byram or Alex Mowatt and they were in the Under 18s just two years ago'. They are our kids and hopefully they will benefit Leeds United for years to come."

With so many established players arriving at the club in the summer of 2014, some of them from abroad, is there a danger of the door to a rapid first team place being slammed shut for products of the Academy?

Neil doesn't see it that way and views the new signings as a challenge to the club's home produced players. He explains: "It doesn't matter who arrives at the club. If you are good enough you will make it into the first team. It is as simple as that. The youngsters have to realise they are in the business of marketing themselves as individuals.

"Although we help in their development they have a responsibility to themselves as well. Football is a cut-throat business. You have to be playing well and being the one who is pushing all the time."

The current group of Under 21s has been together for four years under Neil's supervision and he says they are really gelling as a unit, as well as blossoming as individuals.

The Academy starts with an age nine to 11 foundation stage. Then it's the youth development stage up to age 16 and the pro-development phase from 16 to 21. Neil is especially proud that the 20-strong squad that went to Italy for pre-season training in the summer of 2014 contained 12 Academy players.

During the 2013-14 season, Academy product Dominic Poleon continued his progress as an impact player on leaving the bench, but he was sold to Oldham on deadline day, September 1, 2014. After making his Leeds United first team debut in 2011-12, left back Charlie Taylor went on loan to several clubs and spent the 2013-14 season at Fleetwood. Taylor was outstanding in helping Fleetwood to play-off success at Wembley but returned to Elland Road hoping to secure a regular first team place.

Midfielder Lewis Cook broke into the first team at the start of the 2014-15 season, offering further proof of the Academy's value.

LEWIS COOK

Phil Beeton - United's Super Fan

DEVOTED Leeds United fan Phil Beeton was just five years old when his father took him to see his first Leeds United match.

And towards the end of the 2013-14 season Phil was crowned the country's number one supporter after clocking up more than 2,000 league matches in succession.

It was an amazing achievement and Phil, boss of his family's printing business, was deservedly named Capital One Supporter of the Year at the 2014 Football League awards ceremony in London.

Phil's wife Chris isn't far behind him in the matches-seen count and the couple have spent a fortune following their favourite team through the good and bad times at home and abroad.

United's match-day programme regularly carries photos of keen supporters barely out of their nappies, but how many of them will go on to watch the Whites as many times as Phil?

To mark his 2,000th game in a row, at Bournemouth on Tuesday March 25, the home club treated Phil to a pre-match meal, a visit to the boardroom and a seat in the directors' box. Although United were unable to mark the milestone with a win, as they went down 4-1, Phil enjoyed the occasion and travelled to the match with his branch of the Supporters Club in the normal way.

A few days later he was United's guest of honour at the home Yorkshire derby against Doncaster, which ended in another defeat, though the pill tasted sweeter when he was presented with a five-year season ticket.

"I was quite moved by the award of that five-year season ticket and an autographed shirt which I shall treasure forever," said Phil, who has now spent 50 years as a season ticket holder. "The club, and especially David Haigh, were phenomenal, looking after us 100 per cent. The national award came as a complete surprise. I knew nothing about it until three weeks before the actual event in London.

"I found out that some of my members, and one in particular, had started a campaign and been in touch with the Football League to tell them my 2,000 milestone was coming up. It was an honour for me to be at the awards ceremony and to represent the club. At least we've won something this year," he laughed.

Being blessed with good health and running his own business were big features in helping Phil reach the 2000 mark. He was able to organise his own time off to coincide with the first team's fixtures. Nor was planning trips to away matches a problem as the Supporters Club treasurer has organised travel to away games for his fellow members for many years.

The first match he saw United play was against West Bromwich Albion in the 1957-58 season and he says: "I was hooked straightaway. I enjoyed football from an early age and my father was a keen supporter, so the foundations were there."

He joined the Supporters Club in the 1970s and recalls: "I liked the

organisation and the way they looked after people and got them to games. Then I started organising coaches for one of the local branches. When I left that branch I started one of my own at the Griffin Hotel in the centre of Leeds and the Griffin is still the name of the branch. It is like a family because we have all ages involved and we have a common interest."

Ask Phil what following Leeds United has cost him over the years and he grins: "I don't want to think about it, but I am sure it would have been spent on something else if I hadn't spent it on watching Leeds."

So what is the most memorable match Phil has seen during his love affair with the club? "That would be the game at Liverpool in 1969 when we won the League Championship for the first time," he says without hesitation. "The emotion of that occasion stands out. We had done what we did so well in those days by playing out a nil-nil draw to win the title.

"It wasn't the best of games and as far as I can remember Liverpool were the better team, but we hung in there and the Liverpool fans gave us such a great reception afterwards. I don't think even the players could have imagined that happening.

"Although the two clubs were fierce rivals, there was always mutual respect between them and the two managers, Don Revie and Bill Shankly, were good friends."

Asked to name the best Leeds United player he ever saw, Phil replied: "My father would tell me I should always say John Charles but I was unfortunate in missing the best of John. He had left when I started watching and when he came back in the early 1960s I don't think he was the same player he had been in the 1950s.

"So I would have to go for Billy Bremner, not just for his outstanding playing ability but also for his inspiring leadership. He would go out there with a strain or a broken leg if it helped the cause, have an injection and play for 90 minutes before collapsing in the dressing room."

Phil has no plans to give up his life-long hobby of watching his favourite team. "However good or bad the performances, I would never give up supporting Leeds United," he confirms. "It is in the blood and I love the social side of it as well.

"I've met so many lovely people – not just in Leeds and the surrounding areas, but fans of the team worldwide. I've kept in regular contact with them and when they come over here we always go out for a meal. As I say, it's just like a family."

The first of Phil's 2,000 consecutive league games was at home to Manchester City on March 18, 1967.
The last game he missed was at Southampton on March 4, 1967.

Summing up the squad

Here's a teaser to test your maths and get you familiar with the players' squad numbers.

1 BILLY SHARP **+** NICKY AJOSE **=**

2 GAETANO BERARDI **X** SAM BYRAM **=**

3 TOMASSO BIANCHI **÷** LUKE MURPHY **=**

4 LIAM COOPER **-** STEPHEN WARNOCK **=**

SQUAD NUMBERS: 1 MARCO SILVESTRI, 2 SAM BYRAM, 3 STEPHEN WARNOCK, 4 RODOLPH AUSTIN, 5 GIUSEPPE BELLUSCI, 6 JASON PEARCE, 7 LUKE MURPHY, 8 BILLY SHARP, 9 ADRYAN, 10 NOEL HUNT, 11 AIDY WHITE, 12 GAETANO BERARDI, 13 STUART TAYLOR, 14 TOMMASO BIANCHI, 15 SCOTT WOOTTON, 16 NICKY AJOSE, 18 MICHAEL TONGE,

Using the squad numbers, can you work out these 8 simple sums?
For instance, Noel Hunt wears squad number 10 and Luke Varney wears number 11.
Add them together and your answer is 21.

5 MICHAEL TONGE	**+** JASON PEARCE	**=**
6 LEWIS WALTERS	**−** LEWIS COOK	**=**
7 RODOLPH AUSTIN	**X** AIDY WHITE	**=**
8 ALEX CAIRNS	**÷** GIUSEPPE BELLUSCI	**=**

19 STEVE MORISON, 20 DAVID NORRIS, 21 CHARLIE TAYLOR, 22 ZAK THOMPSON, 23 LEWIS COOK, 24 CHRIS DAWSON, 25 ROSS KILLOCK, 26 BRIAN MONTENEGRO, 27 ALEX MOWATT, 28 LEWIS WALTERS, 29 SOULEYMANE DOUKARA, 30 ALEX CAIRNS, 31 ZAN BENEDICIC, 32 LIAM COOPER, 33 CASPER SLOTH, 34 MIRCO ANTENUCCI, 35 DARIO DEL FABRO.

Perils of being a manager

SO you want to be a football manager. Supporters of most clubs think they could do a better job of picking the team than the man in charge, but the qualities needed to make a successful boss are many and varied.

And as managers are all too well aware, unless they are very, very good at their job or extremely fortunate, the only certainty is that one day they will be sacked.

That's why managers want long contracts, so that if their time in the job is cut short they will be paid compensation.

During the 2013-14 season, Leeds United's Brian McDermott was dismissed and then quickly handed his job back, but his future remained uncertain during the club's change of ownership and eventually he left the club at the end of May, 2014, by mutual consent. He joined the club on April 12, 2013, on a three-year deal, only to fall on his sword less than 14 months later. A head coach was appointed at Elland Road instead of a manager when David Hockaday arrived from Forest Green, but he lasted just 70 days and six matches before losing his job in August, 2014.

All managers accept that their job depends hugely on results and because there are so many teams in every division, very few bosses end up winning trophies.

Stats from Dr Sue Bridgewater, Director of Sports Research at Liverpool University, reveal that in the 2013-14 season, 37 League managers were sacked, including 12 in the Premier League and 10 in the Championship, while 125 coaches lost their jobs. On average, those managers who lost their jobs lasted just under one-and-a-half years.

So if you're looking for a safe occupation, don't go into football management or coaching!

Yet try telling that to the countless managers up and down the country who relish the task of chasing success for their teams.

Sir Alex Ferguson had been in charge of Manchester United for an amazing 26 seasons before he retired at the end of the 2012-13 season and his successor, David Moyes, had been in charge at Everton for just over 11 seasons. But, as we all know, Moyes lasted only a short time before being sacked at Old Trafford, proving that reputations count for nothing if results don't go as planned.

Not all managers who leave their clubs are sacked, of course. Some resign to take on a bigger, more exciting challenge, but the high casualty rate leaves fans asking if clubs are too quick to fire their managers instead of giving them time to build success.

Leeds owner Massimo Cellino said after McDermott left: "Brian is a great manager and a great guy. He has been unfortunate to work in such difficult circumstances. I did not fully understand the mess he had to work in, and the broken promises he had to deal with, until I have got involved trying to turn Leeds around.

"He has been a gentleman to deal with in our discussions and has been very understanding of my wish to implement a new structure. His main concern and priority at all times has been the welfare and protection of Leeds United. I wish him well for the future where I am sure he will continue to have more success and thank him for his efforts in being a stabilising and unifying figure behind the scenes in very difficult circumstances.

"His honest efforts to guide us to the safety of mid-table when faced with many difficulties is appreciated by us all. He will always be a friend of Leeds United."

McDermott said: "It has been my great privilege to manage this great club and I have enjoyed the challenge immensely.

"However it is clear that Massimo wishes to implement a new structure and feels he will work more successfully for Leeds with a coach rather than a manager. I respect that Massimo must be fully supported in putting together his vision for the club so he can bring us the success we all want. It is my belief that when truly United we are stronger. Massimo wants to bring a new energy to the club so that we can return to where we belong as a healthy football club.

"To my players for their efforts I say a big thank-you. To all the staff and especially my great assistant manager Nigel Gibbs and my great friend Patrick Dolan I am especially grateful for their support.

"Finally to the incredible force that is the Leeds United supporters, I offer my heartfelt thanks. Your support of me and the players was always an inspiration and I urge everyone to get behind the team and the new owner next season to get us back to where we need to be, fighting for trophies and competing at the top-table of English and European football.

"It won't be easy, but Marching On Together we can get there. I wish Massimo and all my friends at Elland Road every success in the future."

*Former Leeds United manager Howard Wilkinson paid a warm tribute to Liverpool's Brendan Roders, winner of the League Managers' Association Manager of the Year Award for season 2013-14.

Wilko, chairman of the LMA, said: "Liverpool Football Club's performances and results this season have provoked memories of some of those momentous years in the past when they had to contend with those two Uniteds, the first from Leeds and the second from Manchester."

Longest serving MANAGERS

(Then in their jobs up to May, 2014)
1 **Arsene Wenger** – Arsenal, 17.7 years.
2 **Paul Tisdale** – Exeter City, 8 years.
3 **Mark Yates** – Cheltenham Town, 5.8 years.
4 **Russell Slade** – Leyton Orient, 4.16 years.
5 **Karl Robinson** – MK Dons, 4 years.
6 **Alan Pardew** – Newcastle United, 4.07 years.
7 **Darren Ferguson** – Peterborough, 3.98 years.
8 **Dean Smith** – Walsall, 3.3 years.
9 **Micky Adams** – Port Vale, 2.99 years.
10 **Jim Bentley** – Morecambe, 2.99 years.

Diary of a season 2013-14

ROSS McCORMACK may have left the club for Fulham in the summer of 2014 but his 29 goals in all competitions gave United fans something to celebrate in a season many will want to forget.

From being in a play-off place at Christmas, United suffered an alarming dip in form which could partly be explained by uncertainty over the club's ownership. Manager Brian McDermott found it increasingly difficult to get the right results and at the end of May he lost his job.

The arrival of new owner Massimo Cellino was at first greeted with jeers, but the Italian began to win over the fans and it was no coincidence that results on the field improved once the ownership issue was sorted out.

This is how the 2013-14 season panned out:

August

The biggest first day home crowd since the club's Premier League days – 33,432 – saw Luke Murphy mark his debut with the winner against Brighton from the last kick of the match.

Luke, a £1million buy from Crewe, was one of three United debutants that day. He was joined in the starting line-up by former Reading striker Noel Hunt, while towering ex-Oldham forward Matt Smith was introduced from the bench. McCormack scored a 19th minute equaliser after Leonardo Ulloa had given Brighton a 12th minute lead.

United had never lost a first round Capital One Cup game and recorded a 2-1 home victory over League Two Chesterfield. The Whites trailed but first half goals by Michael Brown and Dominic Poleon saw them safely through.

Rudi Austin, who began the season under suspension, returned to captain the side in a goalless draw at Leicester, which was followed by a 1-1 draw at home to Sheffield Wednesday. McCormack netted United's equaliser after Wednesday had scored from a set-piece.

United fell behind again at Ipswich before winning 2-1 with goals from Luke Varney and McCormack. It was United's first win in their last five visits to Portman Road.

The Capital One Cup second round brought a 3-1 win at Doncaster. Midfielder Alex Mowatt made his debut, aged 17, against his home town club and defender Scott Wootton headed United into the lead on his debut. Former Leeds striker Billy Paynter equalised just after the hour but Smith restored the lead and McCormack added a penalty.

United's first defeat came at home to QPR, Clint Hill scoring the 75th minute goal.

September

Despite a 1-0 win at Bolton, through Varney's sixth minute header, United lost their remaining four matches in September. McDermott's return to his old club Reading was ruined by Adam Le Fondre's goal in added time. United defender Stephen Warnock was sent off for a second yellow card. For Burnley's visit to Elland Road, Sam Byram came in for his first game since April, El-Hadji Diouf was handed his first start of the season and Aidy White made his first league start since April. Smith headed his first league goal for United who lost 2-1 as Burnley gained their first win at Elland Road since 2004.

The Capital One Cup run ended in round three with a 2-0 defeat at Newcastle where a goal in each half won it for the Geordies. It was the same score-line in the league at Millwall who also hit the woodwork three times.

39

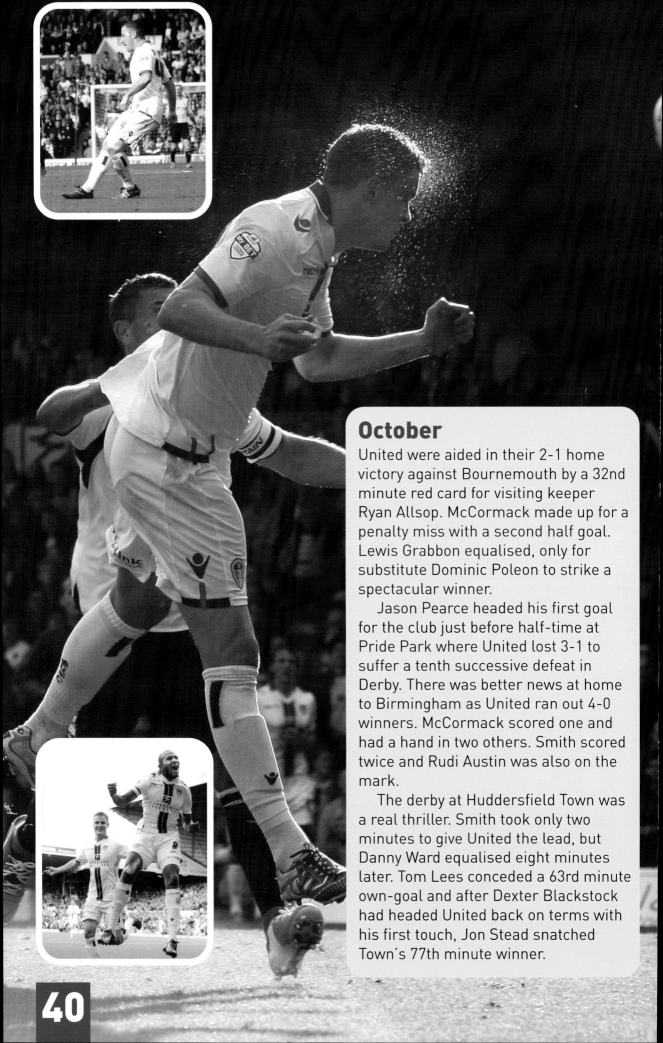

October

United were aided in their 2-1 home victory against Bournemouth by a 32nd minute red card for visiting keeper Ryan Allsop. McCormack made up for a penalty miss with a second half goal. Lewis Grabbon equalised, only for substitute Dominic Poleon to strike a spectacular winner.

Jason Pearce headed his first goal for the club just before half-time at Pride Park where United lost 3-1 to suffer a tenth successive defeat in Derby. There was better news at home to Birmingham as United ran out 4-0 winners. McCormack scored one and had a hand in two others. Smith scored twice and Rudi Austin was also on the mark.

The derby at Huddersfield Town was a real thriller. Smith took only two minutes to give United the lead, but Danny Ward equalised eight minutes later. Tom Lees conceded a 63rd minute own-goal and after Dexter Blackstock had headed United back on terms with his first touch, Jon Stead snatched Town's 77th minute winner.

November

Successive wins over Yeovil Town, Charlton Athletic and Middlesbrough lifted United into the top six. Yeovil had never beaten the Whites and Austin set up the goals for McCormack as United won 2-0 at Elland Road. Stephen Warnock hobbled off, enabling Marius Zaliukas to make his debut. Charlton had gone four games without conceding a goal but McCormack found the net four times in United's 4-2 win at The Valley.

McCormack headed his seventh goal in three games to give the Whites a 35th minute lead at Elland Road against Middlesbrough, the team who had three bids for him turned down in August. Mustapha Carayol got Boro level early in the second half but Jason Pearce conjured up a 57th minute winner to spoil Aitor Karanka's first game in charge of Boro. United were below par at Blackburn where they lost to Tommy Spurr's goal.

December

The year ended with two wins, three draws and a defeat. Wigan's visit brought the Whites' fifth home win in a row as McCormack's brace took his tally for the season to 15. Pearce got the slightest of touches before McCormack's free-kick crossed the line for the second but the goal was credited to United's leading marksman.

United were held to a 3-3 thriller by Watford at Elland Road where the Whites hit back from two down to lead 3-2 before conceding a third with four minutes left. Danny Pugh's goal was his first since October, 2011. Smith scored against Doncaster for the second time in the season as United re-visited the Keepmoat Stadium and triumphed 3-0. McCormack collected his 17th goal of the campaign and his 11th in seven games, and Austin finished off the scoring.

United and bottom of the table visitors Barnsley battled to a goalless draw in Danny Wilson's first game back in charge of The Tykes. Barnsley's Marcus Tudgay was sent off with six minutes left. Lee Peltier's far post header in the first half at Blackpool was his first for the Whites but Tom Ince equalised with a deflected shot. Blackpool's Kirk Broadfoot was handed a last minute red card.

United's unbeaten record in December ended with a 2-1 defeat at Nottingham Forest. Gboly Ariyibi made his debut as a substitute on the hour, with Forest leading 1-0 through Greg Halford's 23rd minute goal. McCormack equalised in the 83rd minute but Matt Derbyshire immediately restored Forest's advantage.

January

This was a frustrating month as poor results and a shortage of recruits during the transfer window hampered progress. It began with a first home defeat since September as Blackburn emerged 2-1 winners, with former Huddersfield striker Jordan Rhodes netting Rovers' opening goal. Rudy Gestede added the second and Smith's eighth goal of the season wasn't enough to rescue the Whites.

A 2-0 home defeat by League Two opponents Rochdale was described by McDermott as his worst moment in football. The nightmare continued at Sheffield Wednesday as the Owls put United to flight 6-0. Smith was sent off and there were debuts for wingers Jimmy Kebe and Cameron Stewart. Connor Wickham, who was on loan from Sunderland and went on to join United on loan later in the season, was one of Wednesday's scorers.

There was a big improvement against table-toppers Leicester City at Elland Road. McCormack took over the captaincy and Varney shone on his recall to the side in his last game before joining Blackburn Rovers.

The run of five defeats ended with a 1-1 draw at home to Ipswich. El-Hadji Diouf made his first start since September, but David McGoldrick gave The Tractor Boys a 57th minute lead and McCormack equalised from the penalty spot.

February

Manager McDermott was 'sacked' and then given his job back on the day United thrashed Huddersfield Town 5-1 at Elland Road with McDermott's assistant Nigel Gibbs in charge. McCormack netted a hat-trick and set up Jimmy Kebe's first goal for the club. Youngster Alex Mowatt scored his first senior goal. A 2-1 win at Yeovil saw McDermott back in the dugout. Ishmael Miller put Yeovil ahead but then lifted a penalty high over the bar. McCormack and Warnock scored wind-assisted goals in the second half.

United lost at Brighton to Leonardo Ulloa's goal soon after the hour. With Paddy Kenny ruled out by an ankle injury, keeper Jack Butland came in on loan from Stoke and had an outstanding debut in a goalless draw at Middlesbrough.

March

Connor Wickham was brought in on loan from Sunderland and made his debut at QPR where McCormack had a penalty saved by Robert Green but then scored with a deflected free-kick. Jermaine Jenas equalised just before half-time. Bolton's visit to Elland Road saw United crash 5-1 for their heaviest home defeat under McDermott's management. Jason Pearce lost his ever-present record as his wife had given birth to a son. Substitute Smith scored in time added on but by then Bolton had put five goals past Butland.

The Whites trailed 4-0 to Reading at Elland Road before restoring some pride with goals from Smith and Austin. McCormack scored at Burnley but the Clarets completed their first double over Leeds for 87 years.

Millwall's visit to Elland Road brought a win at last, with former United hard man turned film star Vinnie Jones introduced to the crowd at half-time. Smith glanced home Wickham's long throw for his 11th goal of the season and McCormack squeezed the ball in from the narrowest of angles for his 26th. DJ Campbell's 72nd minute goal for Millwall set up a nerve-jangling finale but United held on. United crashed to a 4-1 defeat at Bournemouth three days later. It was the first time Bournemouth had beaten Leeds and there were two goals each for Yann Kermorgant and Lewis Grabban. McCormack scored for the third successive game.

After the players agreed to take deferred wages for March, the month ended in a 2-1 home defeat against Doncaster. David Cotterill and Billy Sharp scored first half goals for the visitors, McCormack's goal arriving just after the hour.

April

April Fools' Day was no joke for United who lost 1-0 to relegation-threatened Charlton. The 55th minute goal came from the unpronounceable Remi Ghoochannejhad. McCormack had a penalty superbly saved by Ben Hamer.

United suffered another 1-0 reverse at Wigan where Martyn Waghorn was the Latics' goal-scoring hero. After the match it was announced that Massimo Cellino had succeeded with his appeal against the Football League's refusal to allow him to buy a 75 per cent share of Leeds United.

McDermott's 53rd birthday on April 8 was ruined by a 3-0 defeat at Watford. United's manager described the team's performance as "embarrassing and humiliating".

Successive matches against strugglers Blackpool and Barnsley brought maximum points. United's first win under Cellino's ownership saw two goals from the outstanding Murphy sink Blackpool.

The 1-0 win against Barnsley was United's first at Oakwell since 1977. McCormack's 16th minute goal was his 29th of the season and his 28th in the league. United were chopped down to size at Elland Road by Nottingham Forest striker Matt Derbyshire who struck his first in 92 seconds and his second in the 16th minute.

A 3-1 win at Birmingham raised spirits with Smith, Danny Pugh and an own-goal from Paul Caddis earning United the points, though Mowatt was carried off in added time. In the final game of the season United's improved form was reflected in a 1-1 home draw against Derby. Smith scored United's equaliser. United finished 15th, though a tally of ten points out of 15 was an encouraging finish to a disappointing season in trying circumstances.

Spot the Difference

Can you spot the difference between these two pictures of Nicky Ajose? There are 13 in total. See if you can get them all.

How loan spells made Charlie a better player

CHARLIE TAYLOR was just 17 when he made his Leeds United debut.

Now, after going out on loan to several clubs to gain experience, the York-born left back or winger is keen to hold down a regular first team place at Elland Road after signing a new three-year contract in the summer of 2014.

Life-long Leeds fan Charlie got his big chance when he left the bench in United's 3-2 Carling Cup victory over Bradford City in August, 2011. After another substitute appearance in a 2-1 win at Doncaster in the same competition he made his first league start at home to Crystal Palace on September 10, 2011, again finishing on the winning side as the Londoners were beaten 3-2.

After a brief spell on loan to Bradford City he returned to the club and had to wait until April, 2012, for his next league start, again proving a lucky charm as Peterborough were thrashed 4-1 at Elland Road.

But, faced with a wait for regular first team football at Leeds, Charlie joined his home town club York on loan, making five senior appearances there. Then an opportunity came along to play Scottish Premier League football for Inverness Caledonian where Charlie made eight appearances and learned an enormous amount from former England central defender and captain Terry Butcher.

But it was at Fleetwood, in the 2013-14 season, that he gained the most first team experience, helping them to promotion from League Two under Graham Alexander, earning rave reviews for his performances and turning out 42 times,

including the play-off final against Burton Albion at Wembley.

Not surprisingly, Charlie is a big fan of the loan system and would recommend it to anyone in a similar situation. He said: "Going to Fleetwood definitely improved my game a lot and made me a better player all-round. It helped massively.

"League Two is tough and physical, so it made me stronger, improving my one-against-one defending, which was maybe not the best. All the boys liked the manager Graham Alexander and he helped me a lot. I would advise anyone in my situation to go out on loan like I did to get some experience. It's always better than playing for the under 21s."

The promotion play-off semi-final saw Charlie take on his home town club York and help knock them out. He recalled: "Quite a few of my friends were in the York end cheering them on so I really enjoyed beating York and getting one over on my mates! And of course winning the play-off final against Burton was a wonderful experience."

That was one of the highlights of his fledgling career. Another was turning out for Inverness Caledonian against Celtic at Celtic Park in front of about 60,000 people. "I think it was the day they won the league and the whole stadium was bouncing," he said.

But Charlie's big ambition is to make it at Elland Road. "I will try to hold down a first team place at Leeds this year. That is definitely the plan and hopefully I can do it," he added.

CHARLIE TAYLOR

So-sharp Billy has the answers

BILLY SHARP, who joined United from Southampton just after the start of the 2014-15 season, has had a roller-coaster career, packed with goals but tinged with personal tragedy. In this question and answer session Billy opens his heart to the Leeds United Annual.

Question: What were your feelings on joining Leeds United?

Answer: I was really excited and delighted to be joining Leeds at last.

Q: Did you always have an ambition to play for the club and had they previously shown interest in you?

A: Although I am a Sheffield United fan I've always had a soft spot in my heart for Leeds. I always wanted to play for the club. They were in the Champions League back in the day and fun to watch. The club had shown interest in me a few times but nothing came of it until the deal was finally done a couple of matches into the season.

Q: What were your thoughts on scoring the winning goal against Middlesbrough on your Leeds debut?

A: It was what dreams are made of. I'd dreamed about that for three days. The fans would have been thinking I should have scored with a header a few minutes before but you've got to keep on believing.

Q: When you started out at Middlewood Rovers Junior Club were you a striker and how many goals did you score for them?

A: I was always a striker. I scored a lot of goals at Middlewood but I can't remember how many. My dad could probably tell you that. He played football but not professionally. He was a marathon runner too. Most kids these days want to be like Messi, getting the ball and dribbling with it, but I just wanted to be the one to stick the ball in the net.

Q: You were born in Sheffield but you joined Rotherham's youth scheme before moving to Bramall Lane. Why was that?

A: My dad thought I would get into the first team quicker at Rotherham but it didn't quite work out like that. I had an agreement with Rotherham that I could join Sheffield United and that was brilliant for me because it was my home town club.

Q: Who has been the biggest influence on your career?

A: As a Sheffield United fan I used to look on Brian Deane as one of my heroes and he wished me luck when he found out I was joining one of his old clubs Leeds, but Michael Owen and Alan Shearer are the ones I grew up thinking I would love to be like one day. I managed to meet them both as well, which was really nice.

Q: You had loan spells at Rushden & Diamonds, Doncaster, Nottingham Forest and Reading. What was it like playing on loan?

BILLY SHARP

49

A: My spell at Rushden & Diamonds was a successful one. I didn't really know who they were before I went there but I have fond memories of my time there. I had a good relationship with their fans, which was nice. I had two spells on loan at Doncaster and the first time was probably the better one. Reading got me back playing football, so I was grateful to them, and Nottingham Forest are a big club with a great history. I had a good time there and scored quite a few goals for them.

Q: *You had a very successful partnership at Scunthorpe with former Leeds United striker Andy Keogh. Why do you think you two hit it off so well?*

A: We are a similar age and I remember he was the first person I met at the club. From that day we just seemed to do things together, like eating and going to the gym. We just seemed to click and it was a good time in my career.

Q: *How proud were you to score 30 league goals for Scunthorpe in season 2006-7 and take them into the Championship?*

A: It was a highlight of my career because I broke a club record that had stood for about 70 years. People came close but didn't quite get there, which was nice in a way.

Q: *Did you feel any extra pressure when you were valued at £2million on re-joining Sheffield United from Scunthorpe?*

A: Looking back I think there was extra pressure and it hindered me a bit. I went from Sheffield for £100,000 and went back for £2million when I was still only a young kid. I would have liked that spell at Sheffield to have gone a bit better but there were some enjoyable times like scoring a hat-trick in front of the Kop which was another highlight of my career.

Q: *You were handed the squad number 5 at Doncaster. Did that feel strange for a striker?*

A: It was strange but it was either 5 or 30-something and I thought 5 sounded better. Zinedine Zidane wore 5 once and Lee Sharpe wore 5 once so I was in good company.

Q: *Do you have any superstitions and what is your routine before a match?*

A: I used to have superstitions but I've tried to throw them out of the window now. I have my two little boys on my shin-pads and kiss the image before I leave the dressing room (his two-day old son Luey Jacob sadly died in October, 2011, and his second son Leo Dougie was born in December, 2012). If I've scored the week before, I make sure I eat the same thing the night before the next game. It is usually spaghetti bolognese or chicken lasagne.

Q: *The whole of football was shocked to learn of the death of Luey Jacob. How did you cope with the tragedy and carry on playing?*

A: Football fans helped me through it. They make football special for me. They are the ones who come along and chant your name and keep you going through the good and the bad times. Playing football got me through it.

Dean Saunders was the manager at Doncaster at the time and I rang him after two days of not sleeping, drinking or eating. I asked him if I could play and he said 'yes, definitely' and it was probably the best thing I could have done.

Q: You memorably volleyed a great goal against Middlesbrough just three days after losing Louey Jacob and celebrated by taking off your jersey to show a message which read 'That's for you son'. How emotional was that experience?

A: It was selfish of me in a way, saying I wanted to play, because I hadn't prepared right. When I scored that goal I just wanted to cry and go down the tunnel, but I knew I couldn't do that because I had the rest of the game to play. We lost the game 3-1 in the end but it was a special night that will always live with me.

Q: You and your wife Jade set up the Luey Jacob Sharp Foundation, a charity aimed at raising money for research into gastroschisis and a support network for families affected by the condition. How successful and encouraging has that been?

A: It started off really well. It has been a wee bit frustrating recently because we've been here, there and everywhere, but we are going to try and work hard to kick on again. Research into the condition is so important.

Q: What do you enjoy doing most away from football?

A: I used to play a lot of golf. Going home and watching my boy grow up is funny at the minute because he's a real little character and makes us both laugh a lot.

Q: What is your favourite sport, other than football?

A: I do like snooker. I've managed to get a 9ft table at my house in Sheffield but I've not been able to use it much while I've been moving around. Maybe I'll get more practice now. I do like snooker and golf a lot.

Q: Have you modelled yourself on any player in particular and who is the best player you

have played with?

A: I haven't really modelled myself on anyone but the person I most looked up to was someone I played with at Sheffield United and who also had a brilliant career here at Leeds and elsewhere, Gary Speed. He was a strong guy on the pitch and everyone thought he was strong off it too, but for some reason he's not with us today and that's very sad. My most successful spell was with Andy Keogh at Scunthorpe.

Q: Do you enjoy the fame football brings or does it have its disadvantages?

A: It definitely has its disadvantages but the day that a kid doesn't come up to you for your autograph is the day you know you've lost it and you're not a footballer anymore. If you are driving to the training ground and kids arc at the gates wanting your autograph you feel special.

Q: What was the first car you owned and can you remember how much it cost?

A: A Vauxhall Nova. My dad bought it for £50 off a mate at work. I had it pinched twice and they brought it back twice, so that told me I needed to get a new one!

Q: If you hadn't been a footballer what career would you have followed?

A: I ask myself this question all the time and never get any closer to an answer. At school I had a dream of playing football and I had the dedication to be a footballer. I've had a few teachers writing to me since, apologising for not backing me in my dream and now they say 'well done and congratulations'.

Q: Are you a good time-keeper and are you good around the house?

A: I don't like being late. If I say I'm going to be somewhere at a certain time I'll try and get there five minutes early. You'd have to ask my Mrs if I'm good around the house. I can be better but I do a few bits, yes.

Q: What is your favourite meal?

A: I am always in the mood for steak and I like Sunday lunch with Yorkshire puddings and the lot.

Q: If you could change one thing about yourself what would it be?

A: My curly hair. It takes a lot of work and it does my head in.

Nicky Ajose:
My favourite things

We asked United's former Peterborough striker Nicky Ajose ten questions about his favourite things.

Favourite food?
Calamari. (It's made from squid).

Favourite footballer?
Paul Scholes because he started out as an attacking No10 and with age he dropped back and got even better. Reminds me of Zinedine Zidane.

Favourite holiday destination?
Definitely Dubai.

Favourite team (other than Leeds United)?
It would have to be my home town club Bury.

Favourite sport and sportsperson (other than football)?
Golf and Tiger Woods. I can't play golf myself but I admire Tiger's ability and dedication.

Favourite subject at school (other than sport)?
Geography. I'm good at capital cities and I love travel.

Favourite memory from your childhood?
Playing in a tournament for a local team once or twice a year in Blackpool. It was a weekend trip, I really enjoyed it and we won the tournament.

Favourite person you would like to meet and why?
Barak Obama because he's the most powerful man in the world, so the conversation would be really interesting.

Favourite pastime outside football?
I like watching box sets. I spend hours doing that.

Favourite advice you've been given during your career?
Always work hard. My coaches have told me that from the start and it is the advice I would give to any youngster with ambitions to be a professional footballer.

United's best ever – Do you agree?

WHAT are your favourite memories of Leeds United – their greatest matches, seasons, players, captains and managers?

As part of the celebrations of 125 years of league football, the Football League asked fans of teams all over the country for their nominations, and nearly 100,000 votes were cast through Twitter.

Many of our readers will be too young to have witnessed some of the players, managers, top matches and seasons chosen in the poll, but many videos, DVDs and books have captured the club's magic moments down the years.

So lots of you will be aware of the glory years and the players who became Leeds United legends. Some of the greatest goals have been captured on film and are regularly shown on the big screen at Elland Road before our home matches.

So let's see if you, your parents and grandparents agree with the choices made in the Football League poll. Or maybe you have some suggestions of your own which you can discuss with your family and friends.

Here are the results of the voting by Leeds United supporters:

Best ever MATCH

1 7-0 Southampton (1972)   43%
Dubbed as one of the greatest team performances of its time, including a memorable spell of passing captured on the BBC's Match of the Day.

2 4-5 Liverpool (1991)   17%
An amazing second-half comeback from 5-1 down against the greatest team of that time saw Leeds lamenting a late disallowed goal.

3 2-1 Bristol Rovers (2010)   16%
A promotion winning game that had it all. Leeds had a man sent off and came from behind before local hero Jonny Howson stepped off the bench to equalise, and captain Jermaine Beckford, playing his final game for the club, then scored the winner.

4 Sheffield United 2-3 (1992) 15%
A dramatic Yorkshire derby victory paved the way for Leeds to claim the league title later that day.

5 Bournemouth 0-1 (1990)   9%
Eight years in the second division came to an end on a blazing hot Bank Holiday weekend at Bournemouth.

Best ever MANAGER

1	Don Revie	74%
2	Simon Grayson	19%
3	Howard Wilkinson	7%

BILLY BREMNER

Best ever CAPTAIN

1	Billy Bremner	81%
2	Lucas Radebe	12%
3	Gordon Strachan	7%

Best ever SEASON

1 1991/92   47%
The last Football League champions before the introduction of the Premier League.

2 1967/68   31%
Leeds' first European success under Don Revie.

3 1989/90   9%
The season Howard Wilkinson returned Leeds to the big time.

4 2009/10   8%
Promoted from League 1 after a thrilling end to an enthralling season.

5 2007/08   5%
The season when Leeds came so close.

We're a happy family club

BILL Fotherby, a former Chairman and Commercial Director at Elland Road, never tired of describing Leeds United as a "happy family club."

So it is reassuring that many years later United are among the winners of the Football League's Family Excellence Award for the second year running.

Created in 2007, the Award recognises the outstanding experience provided by clubs for young fans and families as part of the scheme that won the Gold Award at the European Professional Football Leagues' Best Practice Awards during the 2013-14 season.

The judges were especially impressed with the efforts clubs are making to engage with families through match-day entertainment, refreshment facilities and mascot activities.

Shaun Harvey, the Football League Chief Executive and former Leeds United Chief Executive Officer, said: "The Football League Family Excellence Award gives clubs a standard to aspire to when planning their efforts to attract more families and young fans to their matches.

"It is hugely encouraging to see so many clubs receiving the accolade, demonstrating the Football League's on-going commitment to securing the next generation of fans."

A total of 47 clubs across all three divisions of the Football League were given the Award for 2014, the same number as in 2013 despite an increase in the standards being applied by the judging panel. More than ever, Football League clubs are providing family areas and offering exciting match-day entertainment.

Joining Leeds United in receiving the award were:
AFC Bournemouth, Birmingham City, Blackburn Rovers, Blackpool, Bolton Wanderers, Brentford, Brighton & Hove Albion, Bristol City, Burnley, Burton Albion, Carlisle United, Cheltenham Town, Chesterfield, Colchester United, Coventry City, Crewe Alexandra, Derby County, Doncaster Rovers, Exeter City, Huddersfield Town, Ipswich Town, Leicester City, Middlesbrough, Millwall, Milton Keynes Dons, Northampton Town, Notts County, Oxford United, Peterborough United, Plymouth Argyle, Port Vale, Portsmouth, Preston North End, Queens Park Rangers, Reading, Rotherham United, Scunthorpe United, Sheffield Wednesday, Shrewsbury Town, Southend United, Stevenage, Tranmere Rovers, Watford, Wolverhampton Wanderers, Wycombe Wanderers and Yeovil Town.

MIRCO ANTENUCCI

Eddie's top of the class!

ON leaving school, some intelligent and talented young footballers face the difficult decision of whether to go to University or try to build a career in the game they love.

But choosing football ahead of academic studies doesn't necessarily mean kissing goodbye to dreams of University honours.

Leeds United legend Eddie Gray always wanted to be a footballer and with his natural ability that was no surprise. Yet many years after being persuaded by then manager Don Revie to leave his native Scotland and launch a glittering career at Elland Road, Eddie was awarded an Honorary Doctorate of Sport Science by Leeds Metropolitan University in the summer of 2014.

It was the latest in a long procession of awards heaped on the former winger whose popularity throughout the game has long been recognised.

Eddie, who was never booked in a career spanning more than 20 years, was one of the greatest wingers to pull on a Leeds shirt and was likened to Manchester United legend George Best. Between 1965 and 1983 he made over 450 domestic appearances which would have been far more had it not been for serious injuries.

He won the FA Cup, League Cup, FA Charity Shield, Inter-Cities Fairs Cup and the Football League Championship, as well as playing 12 times for Scotland. Eddie went on to become manager of the club and also took charge at Whitby Town, Rochdale and Hull City. In 2000 he was voted the third greatest player in Leeds United's history, behind Billy Bremner and John Charles.

He is a Member of the British Empire and on proudly collecting his Honorary Doctorate in July, Eddie said: "To receive such a prestigious award makes me feel very proud. I'm absolutely delighted for myself, my friends and my family."

Giving advice to the graduating students, Eddie added:

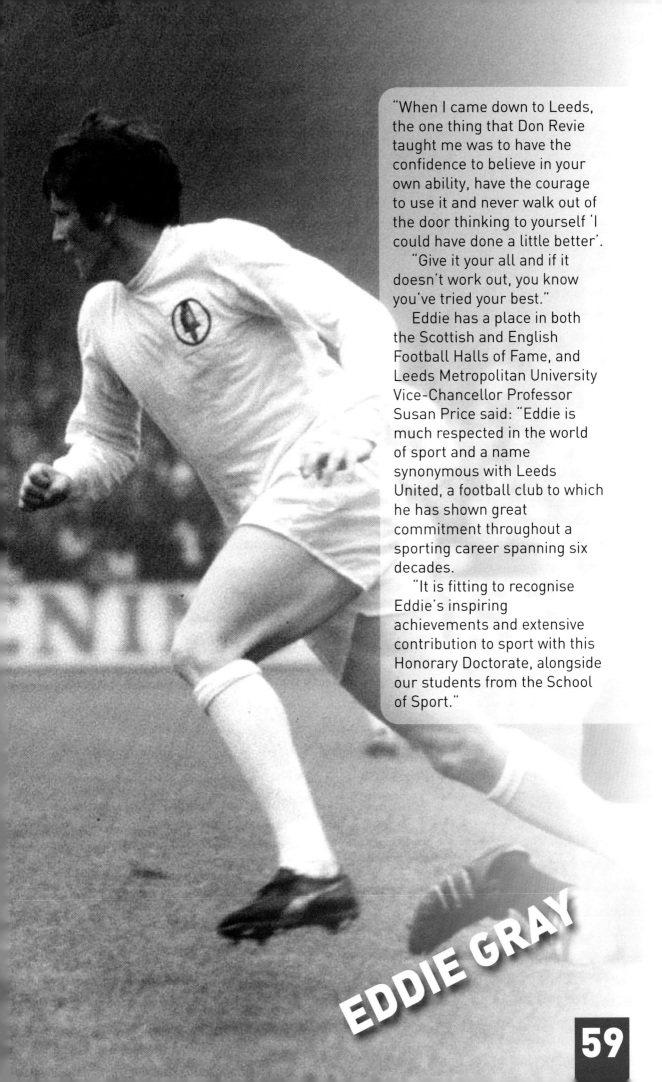

"When I came down to Leeds, the one thing that Don Revie taught me was to have the confidence to believe in your own ability, have the courage to use it and never walk out of the door thinking to yourself 'I could have done a little better'.

"Give it your all and if it doesn't work out, you know you've tried your best."

Eddie has a place in both the Scottish and English Football Halls of Fame, and Leeds Metropolitan University Vice-Chancellor Professor Susan Price said: "Eddie is much respected in the world of sport and a name synonymous with Leeds United, a football club to which he has shown great commitment throughout a sporting career spanning six decades.

"It is fitting to recognise Eddie's inspiring achievements and extensive contribution to sport with this Honorary Doctorate, alongside our students from the School of Sport."

EDDIE GRAY

Have you been paying attention?

YOUR Annual is packed with interesting facts about your favourite club Leeds United. So here are 10 questions to answer and show what you have learned. The answers are on Page 63.

1 What is the name of the Leeds supporter who was named the country's Super Fan in 2014?

2 What club did Souleymane Doukara join Leeds United from?

3 Which former Leeds United player and manager was awarded an Honorary Doctorate of Sport Science in 2014?

4 How many matches did Leeds legend Jack Charlton play for the club in all competitions?

5 Charlie Taylor has been out on loan to several clubs but which team did he help to promotion last season?

6 Who is United's Academy manager?

7 Who headed a goal on his debut against Doncaster in the Capital One Cup second round?

8 Which Leeds United midfielder scored the winning goal on his debut against Brighton on the opening day of the 2013-14 season?

9 Who scored for United in their 1-1 draw against Derby County on the final day of last season, taking his tally to 13?

10 Connor Wickham played five games for United on loan from Sunderland but against which club did he make his Leeds debut?

11 Gaetano Bernardi joined United from which club?

12 Billy Sharp scored 30 league goals in a season for which club?

Find the captains

A	X	H	O	W	S	O	N	M	Y
R	U	O	R	M	S	B	Y	C	K
N	E	S	N	O	D	I	N	A	C
B	A	L	T	C	W	A	B	L	A
U	D	Y	P	I	H	R	R	L	M
T	E	M	L	C	N	A	E	I	R
L	P	O	A	O	B	D	M	S	O
E	V	R	X	S	R	E	N	T	C
R	T	Y	D	I	L	B	E	E	C
S	P	E	L	T	I	E	R	R	M

WE have hidden the surnames of 12 Leeds United captains in this grid of squares. Can you find them? The answers are on Page 63.

LIAM COOPER